The Seed of Eternity

영원의 씨

Lee Won-Ro, Poet / MD / PhD

Published 50 poetry books and 11 anthologies

Hon. Chancellor Inje University Paik Hospitals

Life Member Korean Academy of Science and
Technology

Former President Inje University

Doctor Poet Award

Special Award of the Han Literary Prize

Special Award of the PEN Literary Prize

Distinguished Service Award of Korean Hospital
Association

Distinguished Achievement Prize of Korean Poetry
Monthly

이원로 시인 / 의학박사

시집 50권과 시선집 11권 출간

인제대백중앙의료원명예의료원장

의학박사 심장전문의

한국과학기술한림원 종신회원

인제대학교총장 역임

의사 시인상

한유성문학상 특별상

PEN문학상 특별상

대한병원협회 공로상

월간 현대시 특별상

The Seed of Eternity

The 50th Poetry Book of
Lee Won-Ro

영원의 씨

이원로 제 50 시집

Lee Won-Ro

이원로

Contents

Prologue

Part I
Silence

Silence 20
Poetic Language 22
One More Step 24
Sigh of Relief 26
Judgment 28
Devil's Dance 30
Leaves 32
Roles 34
Hunger 36
May Sunset 38
The Long Way 40

목차

프롤로그

제 1 부
고요

고요 21
시어 23
한 발짝 더 25
안도의 숨 27
심판 29
마귀 춤 31
잎새 33
배역 35
허기 37
오월 해넘이 39
먼 길 41

Part II

Garments of Skin

Starting Point 44
April Rain 46
The Cause and Effect 48
Portion 50
Persistent Curiosity 52
Garments of Skin 54
Smile 56
Derailment 58
Breakthrough 60
The Gate of Eternity 62
Intact Vessel 64

제 2 부
가죽옷

시발점 45

사월 비 47

자초지종 49

몫 51

줄기찬 호기심 53

가죽옷 55

미소 짓기 57

탈선 59

돌파 61

영원의 문 63

온전한 그릇 65

Part III

Approaching Spring

Priority 68
Antenna 70
Approaching Spring 72
The Unseen Light 74
Early Summer 76
Inevitability 78
A Triumphant Entry 80
Dedication 82
Vivacity 84
Forsythia 86
Resignation 88

제 3 부
다가오는 봄

우선순위 69

안테나 71

다가오는 봄 73

안 보이는 빛 75

초여름 77

필연 79

신앙의 여정 81

헌신 83

발랄 85

개나리 87

단념 89

Part IV

Vision

Messenger 92

Switch 94

Departure Whistle Sound 96

Silent Earth 98

Sharing 100

Self-Reproach 102

The Turning Point 104

Someone Somewhere 106

Water and Fire 108

Faraway 110

Vision 112

제 4 부
비전

메신저 93

스위치 95

기적소리 97

말 없는 지구 99

나눔 101

자책 103

계기 105

누군가 어디선가 107

물과 불 109

먼발치 111

비전 113

Part V
Wind and Time

They 116
Last Wish 118
Name 120
Virtual Reality 122
Estimate 124
Eyes of Tomorrow 126
Fairness 128
Wind and Time (1) 130
Wind and Time (2) 132
Intuition 134
Parallel Universe 136

Epilogue

제 5 부
바람과 시간

그들 117

마지막 소원 119

이름 121

가상현실 123

어림 125

내일의 눈 127

공평 129

바람과 시간 (1) 131

바람과 시간 (2) 133

육감 135

평행우주 137

에필로그

Prologue

The Seed of Eternity

Survival and living may differ,
Yet we are all a community
With transcendence and
Commonality as the denominator.

In our hearts, fervent hopes
Always live and wriggle;
In the deepest part of our souls,
The seed of eternity has been sown.

The reason a sincere hope
Persists so tenaciously is
Because there is definitely
A place to run to and achieve it.

The hidden intention of
Planting the seed of eternity
In the depths of our souls
Is undeniably meant to
sprout and bloom it one day.

That is why we will all
Look forward to and run toward
The signal of promise sent
Even on stormy days.

프롤로그

영원의 씨

생존과 생활은 다르지
그러나 우리는 모두
초월성과 공유성을 분모로
어우러진 공동체이지

마음엔 간절한 소망이
언제나 살아 꿈틀대고
영혼의 아주 깊은 곳엔
영원의 씨가 심겼지

진지한 소망이
끈덕지게 버티는 건
달려가 이룰 곳이
분명히 있어 서리

영혼 깊이 은밀히
영원의 씨를 심은 뜻은
언젠가는 틀림없이
씨를 터 피우려 서지

우리는 그러기에 모두
비바람 치는 날에도
보내오는 약속의 신호를
바라보고 달려 나가리

Part I
Silence

제 1 부
고요

Silence

In a heart aimed,
The sound of silence will be heard.
The deeper it is,
The sound will be more profound
and reverent.

In the midst of the silence,
the sound of the beginning will be
heard.
This is the sound of the heart, mind,
and soul taking root.

Within this silence,
What sound are you longing for?
In the profound tranquility,
With whom do I intend to converse?

고요

조준된 마음에는
고요 소리 들려오리
깊으면 깊을수록 더욱
소리는 경건 심오하리

고요 가운데서
태초의 소리 들려오리
마음과 생각과 영혼이
뿌리내리는 소리이지

너는 이고요 가운데서
무슨 소리를 고대하지
나는 깊은 고요 안에서
누구와 대화하려는가

Poetic Language

Poetic language is a splendid
painting
Where each word and phrase come
alive.
It's the voice of a powerful plea.

It must harbor the unique element
that can delve into and stir up
Profound depths where the comforts
and advice of the world are unable
to reach.
Everyone will fall deeply into wonder
and awe when they look at the joyful
smile and the compassionate tear
That are stemming from the very
concise letters recorded in DNA and
RNA through their astonishing
messengers crafted by the magical
combining power.

Everyone aspires to write a poem
That captures even a glimmer of
The enigmatic power of such concise
and condensed language.

시어 詩語

시어는 한 단어 한 어구가
생동하는 멋진 그림이지
강렬한 탄원의 목소리지

세상의 위로나 충언이 못 이르는
깊은 곳을 파고들어 격동시키는
독특한 요소가 간직되어야 하리
DNA와 RNA 안에 기록된 아주
간결한 문자가 신묘하게 결합하여
놀라운 전달물질을 만들어 내고
회로와 시냅스를 매개로 드러내는
환희의 미소와 자비의 눈물을 바라보면
누구나 경이와 경외에 깊이 빠지게 되리

이런 간결하고 농축된 문자의
불가사의한 능력의 한 오라기라도
본받은 그런 시 쓰길 다 열망하리

One More Step

Where are you standing now?
Why are you acting like this?
Pushing aside the fence,
Take one step forward.

What do you see?
Who do you see?
Is it an unfamiliar place?
Is it what you were hoping for?

You did well not to compromise,
You've let go of a great burden by
not being tied down.
Standing at the threshold,
don't be too surprised,
The more you go in, the more
it will be splendid.

Take one more step forward,
There is endless wonder to behold.
You'll be surprised at the place
you'll stand.
You will come to understand why
then.

한 발짝 더

지금 어디 서 있지
왜 그러는 거야
울타리를 제치고
한 발짝 나아가 봐

무엇이 보이니
누가 보이지
낯선 곳인지
기대하던 덴지

타협을 안 하기를 잘했으리
붙들리지 않아 큰 시름 놓았지
문턱에 서서 벌서 그리 놀라지
들어갈수록 더욱 가경일 거야

한 발짝 더 나아가 봐
경탄할 게 무궁무진하지
네가 설 자리에 너도 놀라리
왜 그리되는지 그때는 알게 되리

Sigh of Relief

At the loud cries of cicadas,
The forest will soon fall apart.
Is it a mournful cry to release their
sorrows,
Or a praise for a time gone by?

There may be no set answer.
It depends on the listening ear.

Soon, the burning autumn leaves
Will flutter and cover everything.
Is it the pinnacle of brilliant glory,
Or the spectacle of a sad ending?

There is nothing set in stone.
It all depends on your perspective.

Why do you sigh?
Is it out of admiration or grief?
Whatever the reason,
A sigh will bring relief.

안도의 한숨

매미 소리 요란하다
숲이 온통 떠나가리
한을 푸는 애절한 외침인지
한때를 칭송하는 찬양인지

정해진 건 없으리
듣는 귀에 달렸지

곧 불타는 단풍잎이
온통 날리며 덮으리
찬란한 영광의 극치인지
애석한 종말의 장관인지

정해 둔 건 없으리
보는 눈 나름이지

왜 한숨 짓지
감탄으론 가 비탄에선가
무슨 연유에든
한숨은 안도를 불러오리

Judgment

Dying every day,
Only to be reborn again,
Each day is
A day of judgment.

Even on the day of judgment,
There is comfort and hope.

Fear accumulates,
Sprouting hopes;
The touch of solace
Paves the way for gratitude.

심판

매일 죽고
다시 산다니
하루하루가
심판의 날이지

심판의 날에도
위로와 소망은 있지

두렴이 쌓여
소망을 트리
위로의 손길이
감사의 길을 내지

Devil's Dance

An angel is dancing the devil's
dance.
Why are you so surprised
In a world where devils dance as
angels?

What are they all up to?
They are in the middle of
marionettes.
It's a parade of fashion shows.

They do it because they don't know
that they are angels.
They'll do it because they don't
know that they are devils.
Knowing, but cunning, so they do it.

마귀 춤

천사가 마귀 춤을 추네
뭘 그리 놀라지
마귀가 천사 춤추는 세상인데

무얼 하고들 있는 거지
꼭두각시 공연 중이리
패션쇼 행렬이지

제가 천사인지 몰라 그러리
제가 마귀인 걸 몰라 그러리
알면서도 교활해 그리들 하리

Leaves

Amid the rough winds,
Leaves are greatly shaken.
Are they dancing with joy,
Or trembling in pain?

At first glance, they seem serene,
But upon closer look, it's a quantum
kingdom;
Countless subatomic particles inside
the leaves,
Within them lies an infinite quantum
world.

When leaves shake,
So does the quantum kingdom.
There is infinity inside the leaves,
And perhaps eternity lives within.

In a heavy storm,
The infinity also trembles.
In the midst of a storm,
Eternity also shakes terribly.

잎새

거친 비바람 속에
잎새들이 몹시 흔들리지
기뻐서 춤추는지
아파서 떠는 건지

얼핏 보면 정연한데
자세 보니 퀀텀 왕국이다
잎새 안 무수한 소립자들
그들 속 무한한 퀀텀 세계

잎새가 흔들리면
퀀텀 왕국도 그러나
잎새 안에도 무한이 있고
영원도 그 안에 사는지

비바람 속에 무궁도
몹시 흔들리지
비바람 속에 영원도
몹시 흔들리지

Roles

Swardsmen to gunmen,
Gunmen to swindlers,
They blow away like autumn leaves.

Crying hearts,
Pitiable minds,
Where are they and
what are they doing now?

We are the actors
on the revolving stage,
Turning around in sequence.
The role was not what we expected.

We gaze blankly,
Waiting for the answer
That will come from beyond.

배역

칼잡이는 총잡이에게
총잡이는 꾼들에게
추풍낙엽 신세가 되지

울부짖는 가슴들
안타까운 머리들
지금은 어디서 무얼 하나

순서를 따라 돌아가는
회전무대의 배우들이지
그 배역이 기대에 어긋났지

물끄러미 바라보는
그 너머에서 올
응답을 아직 기다리리

Hunger

Hunger is a difficult fire to tame;
A driving force that lifts us high,
Yet it can also burn us down in
flames.

Time always seems to be on my
side,
Yet time has its own tasks to fulfill,
Living within the confines of
obligations to uphold.

The wind seems to blow for me,
But the wind obeys its own laws
Whether it will cover or clear the
clouds.

Following the gaze of hunger,
Hunger builds the world,
And hunger shatters the world.

허기

허기는 길들이기 어려운 불길
높이 띄워 올리는 원동력이나
화염에 불태워 추락도 시키지

늘 시간이 내 편인 듯 하나
시간도 제 할 일이 따로 있고
지켜야 할 규범 안에 살리

바람이 저를 따라 분다지만
구름을 덮을지 헤칠지는
바람이 따르는 법도 대로리

허기의 눈빛을 따라서
허기가 세상을 세우고
허기가 세상을 부수지

May Sunset

The last subset of May glides over
the green ridge.
Carried by the wind over the hill,
twilight spreads over the meadow.

The leaves and flowers make
unusual gestures with the wind
today.
It must be a special greeting
On their last day.

"What is the last day?
There is no such thing for the wind.
Every step is new,
And it's a different world
when we wake up after sleeping."

Follow the wind,
And when you wake up from sleep,
What is the last?
You will ask yourself too.

오월 해넘이

오월 마지막 석양이
초록 능선 너머로 미끄러지니
구릉을 타고 바람에 실려
어스름이 초원에 깔리지

잎과 꽃들이 오늘따라
바람에 게 유난한 몸짓 하네
마지막 날이라서
특별 인사를 하나 보다

마지막 날이 무어지
바람에 게 그런 건 없는데
가는데 마다 새롭고
자고 나면 딴 세상이지

바람을 따라가 봐
잠을 자고 일어나면
마지막이 뭐지
너도 묻게 되리

The Long Way

The arrogant roar
Of a lion,
A wailing cry
Of a deer caught in a trap.

The cries and roars
Will echo and approach.
The beasts and demons that live
within
Have been whipped and ruled,
And polished carefully.

As long as there is breath
And the blood is flowing,
Is it an indelible flaw?
There is still a long way to go.

먼 길

안하무인 불호령
포효하는 사자이지
울부짖는 비명
덫에 걸린 사슴이지

비명과 불호령 소리
울림 되어 다가오리
안에 사는 맹수와 마귀
채찍질해 다스리며
무던히 갈고 닦았으리

숨이 붙어있는 한
피가 돌고 있는 한
지울 수 없는 흠인지
아직 갈 길이 머네

Part II

Garments of Skin

제 2 부
가죽옷

Starting Point

Even if dark clouds roll in,
Even when a rough wind blows,
Birds are busy eating.

They spin around and peck.
Their heads turn like a machine.
and their beaks move quickly.

The survival instinct mechanism is
more intense and precise than
anything else.
There is nothing more serious in
the world.

It must be the purest obedience
As it is the root that sustains life.
Truly the starting point of
everything.

시발점

먹구름이 몰려와도
바람이 불어 닥쳐도
새들은 먹느라 여념이 없지

주위를 돌며 쪼아먹는다
머리가 기계처럼 돌아가며
부리 동작이 재빠르지

생존본능 메커니즘은
무엇보다 강렬하고 정밀하리
이보다 중한 건 세상에 없으리

삶을 지탱하는 근본이니
가장 순수한 순종 아닌지
진정 모든 것의 시발점이지

April Rain

Carried by a light breeze, it rains in
April;
In the river, in the forest, in the
field, and
Even in the panorama of unfolding
time.
The April rain ripples and draws
something.

Rain clouds roll into the sky.
The wind has already taken its way,
So there will be enough rain to
enrich.
The river will soon gurgle.

The things that come out of
the cocoon are already chosen,
So you shall grow well and prosper.
Don't worry, just run.

Signs of something
Must be already
Stirring inside
As much as outside.

사월 비

미풍에 실려 사월 비가 내리지
　강에도 숲에도 벌판에도
펼쳐지는 시간의 파노라마에도
잔물결 지어 무언갈 그려가지

　하늘로 비구름이 밀려들지
　바람이 이미 길을 잡았으니
풍요할 만큼 충분히 내려주리
강물이 곧 우람하게 굽이치리

　　비집고 나오는 것들은
　　이미 선택된 것이기에
잘 키워주고 번성케 해주리
걱정하지 말고 달려가란다

　　　밖만큼이나
　　　안에도 벌서
　　　무슨 기미가
　　　꿈틀거리리

The Cause and Effect

By doing so,
It has come to this point.

If we continue like this,
We will fall forever.
How can we make it
Turn out like that?
Let's rotate it that way,
So it can be like that.

If we follow that direction,
It will turn out like that.

자초지종 自初至終

그렇게 하여
이렇게 되었다

이렇게 하다간
영영 추락하리니
어떻게 해야
저렇게 되려나
저기로 돌려서
저렇게 해야지

저기에 맞추어가면
저렇게 되어 가리

Portion

Complaining that the portion is
too small,
Grumbling when a share is too
excessive.
Based on the types of portions,
Satisfaction and dissatisfaction will
diverge.

According to the extent of
understanding,
The mind will change.
Not everything is good with
abundance,
Nor is everything bad with scarcity.

Over the distribution of portions,
The world churns and roils.
Discontent closely correlates with
jealousy,
Satisfaction is inversely proportional
to avarice.

This relentless bloody fight to death,
How long will it be dragged on?
Until the sea becomes a teacup,
And the teacup becomes the sea.

몫

몫이 작다고 투정하리
몫이 과하다고 불평하리
몫의 종류에 따라
만족 불만족이 갈라지리

이해의 정도를 따라
마음이 달라지리
많다고 다 좋지 않으리
적다고 늘 나쁜 건 아니리

몫의 분배를 놓고
세상은 출렁거리지
불만은 질투에 비례하고
만족은 시기에 반 비례하리

목숨을 건 피나는 싸움을
언제까지 끌어가려나
바다가 찻잔이 되고
찻잔이 바다가 될 때 까지리

Persistent Curiosity

In the ocean dream shown last
night,
While measuring its depth, sweating
profusely,
I was greatly started by an
encroaching monster.

As the wind blows upward,
But water rushes downward,
It must be a signal to alter direction.
Our insatiable curiosity is striving
eagerly to reveal the unseen.
Who planted that seed within the
heart?
Opportunities come to everyone,
So we try to bloom
that moment of joy.

Everyone runs down that path
Without knowing why
Or what will happen.

줄기찬 호기심

어젯밤 보여준 바다 꿈에서
깊이를 재느라 땀을 빼다가
덮쳐오는 괴물에 무척 놀랐지

바람은 위로 치닫는데
물살은 아래로 달려가니
방향을 돌리라는 신호리
안 보이는 걸 재 내보려
줄기차게 애쓰는 호기심
그 씨를 누가 심장에 심었지
기회는 모두에게 오게 마련이라니
기쁨의 그때를 피워 내려서리

왜 그렇게 되는지
어찌 될지도 모르면서
모두 그길로 내달려가지

Garments of Skin

Because of the fall,
Though driven out,
Garments of skin were dressed.*

Like water spilled upon the ground,
It cannot be contained again,
So they're destined to die.
But some other way was devised
instead of taking their life
immediately.**
It's an amazing plan to rescue them,
When the time is up,
From loitering in the penal colony.

They were guarded impeccably,
Lest they eat the fruit of the tree of
life and live forever as a sinner.

*Genesis 3:21
**2 Samuel 14:14

가죽옷

타락하였기에
쫓아 내면서도
가죽옷을 입혔지*

땅에 쏟아진 물처럼
다시 담을 수 없으니
반드시 죽게 마련이 나
생명을 거두진 않고
다른 방법을 고안했지**
유형지의 배회로부터
때가 차면 건져 올릴
놀라운 계획이지

생명나무 열매 따 먹고
죄인으로 영영 살까 봐
철통같이 지켜주었지

*창세기 3:21
**사무엘 하 14:14

Smile

Everyone is just dust and dirt.
They are grass and flowers that
bloom for a while.
What about the heart and soul?
It may be a crazy virtual reality.

You can't see and catch it
because you're caught in a sigh.
If you smile, it will make a
difference;
It'll open according to the content
of your smile.

If you cross over the fence,
The view opens up.
If you go a little deeper,
You will touch and grasp.

They're grass and flowers
that are blown away,
But they hold eternity inside.
Even when blown away, their pulse
beats inside them,
And when burned, they are
still breathing.

미소 짓기

먼지요 티끌이지
잠시 피는 풀과 꽃이지
마음과 혼은 어쩌지
왁자한 가상현실일지

안 보이고 안 잡히니
한숨에 잡혀서 그러리
미소 지으면 달라지리
미소 내용대로 열려 지리

울타리를 넘어가면
시야가 트여 지리
좀 더 깊이 들어가면
만져지고 잡게 되리

날려가는 풀과 꽃이나
영생을 안에 품었지
날려가도 그 안에 맥박은 뛰고
불에 타도 거기서 숨 쉬고 있지

Derailment

How can all sorrows be the same?
Despair may not be the same for all.
What does your gaze behold?
Whose face does your expression
face?

Don't let you face be downcast.
Don't hang your head low.

It's been a while since the gift was
prepared,
Yet it couldn't be given for your
derailment.
It's been a while since the hand
from above was reaching out,
But it is a pity that you didn't hold
it.

탈선

슬픔이 어찌 다 같으랴
절망도 다 같지 않으리
너의 눈은 무얼 바라보나
너의 얼굴은 누구를 향하지

눈을 깔아 내리지 마라
고개를 떨구지 마라

선물을 챙겨둔 지 오랜데
네가 탈선을 하니 줄 수 없었지
위에서 손을 내민 지 오랜데
네가 안 잡으니 안타까우리

Breakthrough

Every remarkable breakthrough
Serves as an avatar of miracles,
A gift unveiled by the purity
Of believing in miracles.

In every phase of history,
They discover the concealed gifts,
Guiding cultures and civilizations.

The miracles of creation
Still persist through the passage of
time and
Endlessly accomplishing
breakthroughs
To pave the way for significant
advancements.

돌파

모든 비약적 돌파는
기적의 아바타이지
기적을 믿는 순수가
캐내는 선물이지

역사의 단계마다
숨겨둔 선물을 찾아내
문화와 문명을 이끌지

창세의 기적은 아직도
시간의 흐름을 타고 살며
큰 발전의 계기를 마련할
돌파를 끝없이 이루어가지

The Gate of Eternity

Your smile
Becomes my joy,
And that smile and joy
Become our strength.

Your vision
Becomes my hope,
And that vision and hope
Become our future.

Your love
Becomes my faith,
And that love and faith
Open the gate of eternity.

영원의 문

당신의 미소가
나의 기쁨이 되고
그 미소와 기쁨이
우리의 힘이 되지

당신의 비전이
나의 소망이 되고
그 비전과 소망이
우리의 미래가 되지

당신의 사랑이
나의 믿음이 되고
그 사랑과 믿음이
영원의 문을 열지

Intact Vessel

Everyone hopes to be filled;

Desires, pleas, and hopes
Soar forth to be fulfilled.

With what do you wish to be filled?

Filling the void, filling the hunger,
Even when poured and filled, it
remains vacant.

How do I seek fulfillment?

Is it not pouring into a leaky vessel?
Am I pouring something that will
evaporate?

What do you want to pour into what
vessel?

온전한 그릇

모두는 충만 되길 바라지

욕구와 간구와 소망이
충만을 위해 솟구치리

너는 무엇으로 충만하려나

빈자리 메우기 허기 채우기
부어도 메워도 차지 않으리

나는 어떻게 충만하려나

밑 빠진 독에 붓는 건 아닌지
증발해 사라질 걸 붓고 있는지

어떤 그릇에 무얼 부으려나

Part III
Approaching Spring

제 3 부
다가오는 봄

Priority

What is your ultimate priority?
No need to ponder deeply to extract
it.
It's already etched in your DNA.

No matter how much you wander
the world,
Even if you burn yourself out entirely,
In the end, you'll reach what's been
put within.

Wandering, rebellion, and obedience
Will all proceed according to plan.
As it is written, so be it.

우선순위

너의 최 우선순위는 무언가
고심하여 캐낼 것까지 없지
DNA에 이미 새겨져 있지

아무리 세상을 돌고 돌며
심신을 다해 불태웠어도
결국 넣어준 거기에 도달하지

방황과 거역 순종 모두
예정대로 진행 되어 가리
써진 글씨대로 그렇게 되리

Antenna

You and I are mutual exploratory
antennas;
Observing and tracing,
Discovering and responding,

To grasp the situation that unfolds.

You and I are complementary
antennas;
Imitating and adjusting,
Perceiving and supplementing,

To make us aware of deficiencies
and excesses.

We are mutual empathetic antennas;
A field of comfort and
encouragement,
A realm of hope and trust,

To write the history of preservation.

안테나

너와 나는 상호 탐색 안테나
감시하며 추적하고
알아내고 대응하리

국면을 파악하려 서지

나와 너는 상호 보완 안테나
모방하며 조정하리
파악하여 보충하리

부족과 과잉을 알게 하려 지

우리는 상호 공감 안테나
위로와 격려의 장
소망과 신뢰의 장

보전의 역사를 쓰게 하려 지

Approaching Spring

Beyond the distant mountain ranges,
All focus their gazes and incline
their ears.
What's to come is definite, but when
is uncertain.
Anticipation magnifies the joy it
brings.

We live In a world where everyone
fences off each other and claims
territorial rights,
But approaching spring will become
a realm of sharing.
Gathering bodies, hearts, and souls
together,
It will be the season that catches
the signals sent.

Park keepers, along the water's
edge,
Plant spring amid sweat and toil.
As they sow outside, so shall it grow
within.
Each piece comes together to form
a splendid symphony.

다가오는 봄

먼발치 산 너머로 모두
시선 집중하고 귀 기울이지
올 건 분명한데 언젠진 모르지
기다림이 기쁨을 증폭시켜주리

누구나 서로 울타리치고
소유권을 주장하는 세상이나
다가오는 봄은 공유의 장이 되리
몸과 마음과 혼을 함께 모아
보내오는 신호를 잡는 계절이지

공원 지기들이 물가를 따라
땀을 흘리며 봄을 심어 가지
밖에 심는 대로 안에서 자라가리
한가락씩 모여 멋진 교향악이 되지

The Unseen Light

Is this really what darkness is like,
A stage filled with unseen light?
Is this really what fear feels like,
An era when the light of love
cannot be seen?

As the black and white world
fades away,
A brilliant world draws near.
As the unseen light reveals itself,
The unseen world unfolds before us.

Old and faded thoughts and hearts
Will dress up in emerging bright
shine,
Growing larger and expanding,
Rushing towards infinity in stride.

안 보이는 빛

어둠이 진정 이런 건지
안 보이는 빛이 차 있는 무대
두렴이 실로 이런 건지
사랑의 빛이 안 보이는 시대

흑백 단순 세상이 사라져가며
휘황찬란한 세상이 다가오지
안 보이던 빛이 드러나며
못 보던 세계가 열려가리

낡고 바랜 생각과 마음이
드러나는 새 빛으로 단장하고
점점 커지며 넓어져 가리
무한을 향하여 달려가리

Early Summer

Summer is approaching already,
While the tales of spring are still in
disarray.

What's coming is the time of
meetings,
Expectations swell, causing hearts to
flutter.
What's departing are promises made,
Turning into cherished memories to
reminisce.

All that's blossoming forth
Are beautiful hopes.

In our hearts where
early summer blooms,
The things we've longed for
will compete
To draw a dazzling future.

초여름

여름이 다가오지 벌써
봄 사연이 아직 어수선한데

오는 건 만남의 시간
기대 부풀어 가슴 설레리
가는 건 약속의 다짐
회상으로 필 추억이 되리

피어나는 건 모두
아름다운 소망이지

초여름이 피어나는
우리의 가슴 안에서
고대하던 것들이 다투어
눈부실 미래를 그려보리

Inevitability

My heart is ablaze,
But my hands cannot reach.
What can I do?
This moment passes in vain.
Will it be forgotten,
A fleeting accident,
With no one to know,
No record to keep?

The eyes of chance are always
Anxious and empty.
The eyes of inevitability are always
Confident of victory.

Even if it looks like that,
Even if it feels like that,
But someone knows,
It is recorded somewhere.
Because it is a noble passion,
No matter what it looks like,
It has already worn the laurel wreath.

필연

가슴에는 불길이 오르지만
손길이 못 미치니 어찌하리
아깝게 안타까이
스쳐 가는 이 순간
아무도 모르게
기록도 없이 흘러가는
잊혀 질 우발사건인지

우연의 눈은 늘
초조하고 허망하리
필연의 눈은 항상
승리를 확신하지

그렇게 보이지만
그처럼 느껴지지만
누군가는 알고 있지
어딘가엔 기록되었지
숭고한 열정이기에
겉보기론 어찌 되었든
월계관을 이미 썼지

A Triumphant Entry

The journey of faith is
A mysterious
Path of planning, execution, and
fulfillment,
Leading to glory;
The expedition of a triumphant
entry.

Appointment, predestination, calling
Justification, sanctification,
And glorification.

Awe and reverence,
Mystery and miracles,
Eternity and boundlessness,
All emerge from here
And return here.

승리의 입성

신앙의 여정은
불가사의한
계획과 실행과 완성
영광에 이르는
승리의 입성 원정이지

작정 예정 부름
칭의 성화 영화

경이와 경외
신비와 기적
영원과 무궁
모두 여기서 나오고
여기로 돌아가지

Dedication

Dedication is not a game played
in pursuit of rewards alone.
The bounty may be of unknown value,
and the timing uncertain,
Yet it can exist even with nothing to
gain.

**In the flow of time and trends,
The meaning and understanding of
devotion change.
I am afraid that my devotion is
outdated.**

However, genuine dedication is
A path of challenge
That is driven by a great power
That cannot be rejected
or disobeyed.

**The deception within is
More painful
Than the evil without.**

헌신

헌신이 보상금을 따러
달려드는 게임은 아니리
현상금이 얼마이고
언제일지도 모르리
아무것도 없을 수 있으리

시대에 실려 추세를 따라
헌신의 의미도 이해도 바뀌니
시대착오적 헌신일까 두렵지

그러나 신실한 헌신은
뿌리칠 수 없고
거역할 수 없는
큰 힘에 끌려
달려가는 도전의 길이지

밖의 사악 보다
안의 현혹이
더 아픈 걸림돌이 되리

Vivacity

Today's me
Is not yesterday's me,
And tomorrow's me
Will be different from today.

Today's dream
Differs from yesterday's dream,
How could tomorrow's dream
Be the same as today?

Because we are always
full of vivacity,
We will reach perfection
full of joy and
Full of expectations.

발랄

오늘의 나는
어제의 나가 아니고
내일의 나는
오늘과 다르리

오늘의 꿈은
어제의 꿈과 다르고
내일의 꿈이 어찌
오늘과 같으랴

언제나 발랄하기에
기쁨 가득히
기대에 넘쳐
완성에 이르리

Forsythia

Riding on a sunny current,
A lively dance unfolds.
Soaked in the April rain,
sprouts emerge,
Leaves and flowers poised to bloom,
But the spring breeze is fierce this
year.

Already, the feeble forsythia blooms,
Swinging wildly in the chilly wind,
"Isn't it too early to come out?" I ask
out of feeling pitiful and sorry,
And they reply, "Do you know
who sent the signal?
You are so full of doubts!
That's why you can't even take
a step forward."

In my heart, which was once empty,
Timely rain will soon flow in and fill
it up.
As my heart swells,
My mind will also bloom,
And I will meet my time
in the world.

개나리

화창한 기류를 타고
발랄한 춤이 벌어지리
실비에 젖어 싹이 트고
잎과 꽃이 피어나려는데
올 따라 꽃샘바람이 매섭지

벌써 핀 가냘픈 개나리가
찬바람에 마구 휘둘리지
"너무 일찍 나온 거 아냐?"
딱하고 안쓰러워 물으니
"누가 보낸 신호인지나 아니?
너는 정말 의심도 많구나!
그래서야 한발 앞도 못 내딛지."

밑바닥이 드러나던 가슴에
단비가 곧 흘러들어 채워가리
가슴이 부풀어 오르면
머리도 덩달아 피어나지
제구실할 때를 맞게 되리

Resignation

The sky collapsed and he was
stunned.
Even so, he has a knack for
resignation, and decides to
accompany terminal cancer as a
friend.

Where does such talent come from?
It must be a gift given to the wisdom
of decision,
The belief that there's always
something next.

In transitional seasons, everywhere,
There are always unexpected storms,
Hoping that resignation remains
unshaken.

Resignation is not surrender,
It's a wise transcendental choice,
That cannot be measured or
debated.

단념

하늘이 무너지는 아연실색이나
그래도 단념하는 재주가 있어
말기 암을 친구로 모시며 동행한단다

그런 재주는 어디서 나오는가
결단의 지혜에 주어지는 선물이겠지
다음은 어디나 있다는 믿음이지

환절기에는 어디에나 늘
예기치 않은 풍파가 있으니
단념이 흔들리지 않길 바라지

단념은 항복이 아니라
자로 재고 따질 수 없는
현명한 초월적 선택이지

Part IV
Vision

제 4 부
비전

Messenger

What do you gaze upon?
It's the swollen branches,
Blossoming buds;
What do you hear?
Is it the sound of flowing water,
Or the approaching footsteps?

Within the intricately woven circuitry
And synaptic network of the
messenger,
The universe will operate in a
wondrous way.

The messenger will approach
unhindered by time, place, or
person,
We await the messenger today too,
Whose message remains unknown,
Filled with anticipation and curiosity.

메신저

무얼 바라보나
부푸는 가지이지
피어나는 봉오리지
무엇이 들리지
흐르는 물소리냐
달려오는 발소리냐

정교히 얽힌 메신저의
회로와 시냅스 망 안에서
우주는 놀랍게 운행되리

때나 장소나 누구나를
가리거나 개의치 않고
오게 될 전령은 다가오지
무엇을 전달할지 모르는
메신저를 오늘도 기대와
호기심에 차 기다리지

Switch

Every day, the fog thickens,
And clouds cover the sky,
Yet, spring rain doesn't fall.
How mistakenly we've seen
fine dust and yellow haze
As rain clouds.

Clearly, we don't even know
That we have been caught
in illusions;
Captivated by the specter,
How can we look ahead?

Without plugging the cord into
the socket,
Or plugging it into a broken outlet,
Unaware that the cord is severed,
Even if we push the switch,
How can we expect our desires to
materialize?

스위치

매일 안개가 자욱하고
구름이 하늘을 덮는데
봄비는 내리지 않는다
미세먼지 황사를 어찌
비구름으로 헛보았지

몰라서 그러리 분명
무언가에 씌워있어
허깨비에 잡혀 있으니
어찌 앞을 내다보리

소켓에 줄도 안 꼽고
고장 난 데 잘 못 끼우고
줄이 끊어진 것도 모르며
스위치를 다그쳐봐야
바라는 게 어찌 일어나리

The Departure Whistle Sounds

Yesterday and today were
full of suffering,
Tomorrow is unpredictable.

I toss and turn
In the sleepless night.

At the resounding departure
whistle sounds,
My heart is broken.

Who is calling me?
What are they telling me to do?

출발 기적소리

고난의 어제와 오늘
예측할 수 없는 내일

이리저리 뒤척뒤척
잠 못 이루는 밤

울려오는 출발 기적소리에
억장이 무너지지

누가 부르는 소리지
무얼 하라는 소리지

Silent Earth

The day was bright,
But the sunlight was dim because it
was covered in fine dust.
Spring is approaching, but
We must watch a little longer
To see what wind will blow.

When the things frozen in the winter
wind
Start to stand tall and adjust their
stance,
You can even hear the sound of the
stream.

Carrying enthusiastic crowds,
Burdensome crowds,
And timid crowds,
The earth silently cuts through
the wind and dust on its given orbit.

말 없는 지구

날은 밝았는데
미세먼지에 가려
햇빛은 희미하지
봄은 다가오는데
어떤 바람이 불어올지
좀 더 지켜봐야 하리

겨울바람에 얼었던 것들이
자세를 고쳐 세워갈 때면
냇물 소리도 제법 들려오지

열광하는 무리
버거워하는 무리
겁내는 무리를 태우고
지구는 말없이
바람과 먼지를 헤치며
주어진 궤도를 달리지

Sharing

Even if the path is cut off,
Even if the door is closed,
Even if you are trapped in darkness,
Sharing will banish loneliness.

Even on a brilliant stage,
Even standing tall in the midst of
applause,
Even in the vortex of cheers,
If there is no sharing, there is
loneliness.
The window of conversation is
always open,
And hands are extended everywhere,
But if the five senses are buried in
oneself,
They will sink into the sea of
loneliness.

Loneliness is a sharing deficiency.
The soul dries up, the bones melt,
The brain withers and crumbles,
It will become the root of all
diseases.

If you often pretend to share,
It will become as you wish.
Do not be ashamed to extend your
hand.
You must grab the rope that is
lowered.

나눔

길이 끊겼어도
문이 닫혔어도
어둠에 갇혔어도
나눔이 있으면 고독은 없으리

찬란한 무대에서도
갈채 가운데 우뚝 서도
환호의 소용돌이 안에도
나눔이 없으면 고독하리
대화의 창은 늘 열려 있고
어디서나 손을 내미는데
오관이 자기 안에 파묻혀
고독의 바다로 침몰해가리
고독은 나눔 결핍증
혼이 메마르고 뼈가 녹지
뇌수가 시들어 부서져 가지
만병의 근원이 되리

나누는 시늉을 자주 하면
원하는 대로 그리 되어 지리
손 내밀기를 부끄러워 마세
내려주는 줄은 붙잡아야지

Self-Reproach

With blame
And curses,
I accuse and
Foam at the mouth.

In the end, all blame is
a form of self-criticism.
It is an expression of
One's own dissatisfaction
With one's own mistakes.

The performance of rebuke and
reproach that I have staged outside
Will come back to haunt me through
the circuit of self-reproach.

However, excessive self-blame is
truly self-punishment.
It is the dark rebellious force
that pretends to be the master.

자책

비난으로
저주하며
죄를 씌우고
거품을 물지

그러나 모든 책망은
실은 자기 잘못에 대한
자기의 불만의 토로
자기 질책의 모습이지

자기가 밖에 펼쳐낸
책망과 비난의 연출은
자책의 회로를 타고
저를 다시 다그치지

그러나 지나친 자책은
진정 자기 징벌이지
제가 주인 행세하는
어두운 반항적 세력이지

The Turning Point

For what turning point
Does the comet soar
Towards the sun?

To become like the light,
It will burn its body,
As it approaches and cries out.
To breathe freely,
It will plead as it orbits.

Suffering is the beginning of
realization.
Pleading is the first step to
permission.
Withstanding is the turning point
of achievement.

계기

무슨 계기를 마련하려
혜성은 태양을 향해
솟구쳐오르려는가

빛과 같이 되고 싶어
몸과 마음을 태워 가리
다가가며 울부짖으리
자유로이 숨 쉬고 싶어
궤도를 돌며 호소하리

고난이 깨달음의 시작
간청은 허락의 첫걸음
버팀이 성취의 계기이지

Someone Somewhere

Devotion

Is it a good thing
to be absorbed in something?
Or is it just sweating and bleeding?
It's a pity.
Everyone here doesn't know,
But someone somewhere must know.

Risk

Is it worth risking your life?
Is it like walking on thin ice?
Is it the right thing to do?
Or is it a ridiculous ?
No one says anything,
But someone somewhere will surely
know.

Tightrope Walking

Jumping on a rope and doing stunts,
They fall from time and space.
Is it a good thing to do?
Or is it a reckless act?
Even if no one shows any expression,
Someone somewhere must know.

누군가 어디선가

몰두하는 일
잘하는 짓인지
피땀만 흘리는 건지
안타깝다
여기선 모두 모르지만
누군 간 어디선 간 분명 알리

목숨 거는 일
살얼음판 건너는 짓
제대로 하는 노릇인지
우스꽝스러운 게임인지
아무도 말 안 하나
누군 간 어디선 간 분명 알리

줄 타고 묘기 부리다
시공에서 추락하지
잘하는 짓인지
무모한 소행인지
아무 표정 없어도
누군 간 어디선 간 분명 알리

Water and Fire

From the dead branch
The buds that had been hidden deep
Push out their heads, shedding their
skin.

The branch, swollen with rain,
Gleams even brighter in the unusual
sunlight.

That which was so hard
Has melted and dissolved
surprisingly.
Something must have happened
that was beyond imagination.

It is a gift that is hard to bear,
Poured into the heart of patience.

Because a desirable tomorrow is
glimpsed,
That which had been pushed to the
edge of a cliff
Has been revived by water and fire.

물과 불

죽었던 가지에서
깊이 숨겼던 망울들이
껍질을 제치고 눈을 내밀지

실비 세례로 부푼 가지가
유난한 햇살에 더욱 빛나지

그처럼 단단하던 게
놀랍게 녹아 풀어지니
엄두 못 낼 일이 있었으리

참는 마음에 부어 넣어주는
감당키 어려운 선물이지

바람직한 내일이 엿보이기에
낭떠러지 끝에 밀려 있던걸
물 주고 불 지펴 살려내었으리

Faraway

The greatest hope is
the hope from far away.
The deepest prayer is
the prayer from far away.

Not daring to approach,
Hiding behind and bowing one's
head,
It is a tearful appeal,
believing in grace.

Daring not to hope for it,
Not truly deserve it,
It is a prayer of the soul,
believing in miracles.

먼발치

먼발치 소망이
가장 큰 소망이지
먼발치 기원이
가장 깊은 기원이지

다가서지도 못하고
뒤에 숨어 고개 숙여
은혜를 믿고 드리는
눈물의 호소이지

감히 바랄 수 없어
진정 자격이 없기에
기적을 믿고 드리는
영혼의 간구이지

Vision

Beyond the distant mountains,
across the sea,
Above the lofty sky,
Everything in the world
Comes from there and goes there;
Meetings and partings,
Dreams and love,
Descend from there and
reap from there.

An immeasurable vision
of wonder and awe
Will come from there;
A land with no end but only a
beginning,
No emptiness but only fullness,
No darkness but only light.

There is always
Joy and peace,
Bubbling with vitality,
In this everlasting kingdom.
Holding that vision deeply,
Without hesitation, full of joy,
I will run into the great hope.

비전

먼 산 너머 바다 건너
드높은 하늘 위
세상의 모든 건
거기서 오고 거기로 가지
만남도 헤어짐도
꿈과 사랑도
거기서 내리고 거두리

헤아릴 수 없는
경이와 경외의 비전이
거기서 다가오리
끝은 없고 시작만 있는
공허는 없고 충만만 있는
어둠은 없고 빛만 있는 나라

거기는 언제나
환희와 평화가
발랄하게 넘치는
영원무궁의 왕국이지
그 비전 깊이 간직하고
거리낌 없이 기쁨 가득
큰 소망 안으로 달려가지

Part V
Wind and Time

제 5 부
바람과 시간

They

They are naturally
Quick to be afraid;
For fear that the earth will collapse
Or that the sky will fall.

They are by nature
Likely to rush in recklessly.
Are they too clever
Or too foolish?

Nevertheless, it is surprising
Why someone is with them,
Embraces them, protects them.
And keep them alive.

그들

그들은 본시
지레 겁을 잘 내지
땅이 꺼질까 봐
하늘이 무너질까 봐

그들은 본래
무모하게 달려들리
지나치게 영리해선가
너무 우둔해선가

그럼에 도 불구하고
함께 해주고 지켜주며
품어서 살려가니
왜인지 놀라울 뿐이지

Last Wish

Just before I leave here,
If someone asks me what my last
wish is,

Will my thirsty instinctual desire
Burst out of me shamelessly?
Will I pause and stop thinking,
And look up at the sky?

Depending on whose favor it is,
The answer will vary greatly:
From the longing for an eternal
tomorrow
To a delicious drink.

Is the last wish
truly the last?
Is hope still necessary
even in paradise?

As long as there is life,
there is hope.
Hope is life itself.

마지막 소원

여기를 떠나기 직전
마지막 소원을 묻는다면

갈급한 본능적 욕구가
염치없이 터져 나올지
멈칫 생각을 멈추고
하늘을 우러러 바라볼지

누구의 호의인지 따라
대답은 천양지차 이리
영원한 내일의 갈망서부터
맛 좋은 술 한잔까지 이리

마지막 소원이 진정
마지막 일가
낙원에서도 희망은
계속 필요한 건지

생명이 있는 한 희망이 있으리
희망이 곧 생명 자체이지

Name

Having laid down all things,
What will the future be like,
That we have accepted,

How did we receive this name,
But we put it all down,
Was it the name given to dedicate?

In that future,
Will we live without a name,
Or will we receive a new name?

The future is beyond our
understanding,
Why do we still try to pry it open?
Is it because we are still attached
to our names?

이름

모든 걸 내려놓고
받아들인 미래는
어떤 것인지

어떻게 받은 이름인데
이마저 다 내려놓지
바치라고 준 이름이었나

그 미래에서 우리는
아무 이름 없이 살지
새로 이름을 받을지

인지를 초월한 미래인데
억지를 쓰며 캐려느냐
아직 이름에 애착이 있어서지

Virtual Reality

In the past, the sky was filled with
kites,
Today, the universe is explored by
spaceships.
What will rise and fall tomorrow,
Where and what will happen, only
time will tell.

Within time, there is space,
Space lives within time.
Space is time,
All of this is virtual reality in the
brain.

The eyes running beyond,
The wind blowing from there,
Seeing them make a commotion,
It seems it's not just an illusion.

가상현실

그때는 연이 날리던 하늘
오늘은 우주선이 헤치는 우주
내일은 뭐가 오르내릴 건지
어디로 뭘 어찌할지 시간만 알리

시간 안에 공간이 있지
공간 안에 시간이 살리
공간이 바로 시간이란다
모두 뇌 안의 가상현실이지

너머로 달려가는 눈
거기서 불어오는 바람
법석 떠는 걸 보니
환상만은 아닐 상 싶다

Estimate

Having learned to win by embracing,
The next door has opened for me.
So standing in the fading field,
I will be able to hug the rising
starry world.

Even in front of the heavily guarded
wall,
I will look over there with a needle's
eye,
Estimating the universe with
a particle.
I'll figure out who I'll meet and
what I'll do.

As the ritual goes step by step,
The baptism of fire will soon begin.
Where and how will the records of
memories and imagination be stored?

A smile will appear
On the elegant face.
It will be a wonderful place
and a good time,
All the year round.

어림

받아들이는 법을 배워
다음 문이 열렸기에
땅거미 지는 벌판에 서서
떠오르는 별나라를 안으리

경계 삼엄한 장벽 앞에서도
바늘귀로 저쪽을 살펴보며
미립자로 우주를 추정하지
누굴 만나 뭘 할지 어림해보리

한 발짝씩 다가가면서
불꽃 세례가 곧 시작되리
기억과 상상의 기록들은
어디에 어찌 담겨 지지

우아한 얼굴에
미소가 담기리
멋진 곳 좋은 때리
사시사철 그러리

Eyes of Tomorrow

The dreary tunnel of early spring
Is painted in bright colors.

Everyone is taking pictures,
Trying to capture the fleeting
moments.

The April sky is the backdrop,
And the flowers and hearts are
the stage.
Who will you send it to?
Where will you be next year?

The heart to cherish is the eyes of
tomorrow.
A panoramic view is the world of
hope.

I will pass through the tunnel of
night, illuminating it
With the dazzling colors engraved.

내일의 눈

음산하던 초봄의 터널을
화사한 빛깔이 칠해 가지

만개의 한때를 잡아 간직하려
너 나 할 것 없이 사진찍기다

사월 하늘이 배경이고
꽃과 마음이 무대이지
누구에게 어디로 보낼 거지
내년엔 누구와 어디서일지

간직하는 마음은 내일의 눈
내다보는 전경은 소망의 세상

눈부신 빛깔을 담고 새겨
밤의 터널을 밝혀 지나가리

Fairness

I have tried so hard,
With prayers, thoughts, and
attempts,
But if it is not allowed to open,
How can I open it?

Is the opportunity for blessing
Fair to everyone, everywhere?

In the name of realizing a noble
ideal,
The place that was opened to be
shared
Has somehow turned into
Their own nests,
With fences around it.

He will truly open it and let it go,
But how can we stop the desire to
monopolize it?

공평

간구와 궁리와 시도로
무던히도 애쓰지만
허락되지 않는다면
어찌 열 수 있으리

누구에게나 어디서나
축복의 기회는 공평한지

숭고한 이상을 실현한다 해
나누라고 열어준 곳은 어느새
제가 꾸민 보금자리로 변하지
철책이 겹겹이 둘려가고 있지

진정 충분히 열어 내려주지만
독차지하려는 마음을 어찌하지

Wind and Time (1)

Wind is a ride,
Look at the soaring kite.
Don't fight it with your wings.

Time is a ride,
See the winding river.
Don't try to force it back.

Wind is a companion,
Look at the dancing trees.
If you charge it recklessly,
it will break.

Time is a companion,
See the sun's orbit.
Deviating from orbit is a fall.

바람과 시간 (1)

바람은 올라타는 거야
높이 떠가는 솔개가 보이지
날갯짓으로 싸울 게 아니지

시간은 올라타는 거야
굽이치는 강이 보이리
되돌리려 억지 쏠게 아니리

바람은 사귀는 거야
춤추는 우듬지를 보라
무모하게 덤비면 꺾이리

시간은 사귀는 거야
태양의 공전이 보이지
궤도 이탈은 추락이지

Wind and Time (2)

Wind is like time,
Blowing from somewhere
to somewhere else.

Time is like wind,
Flowing from when
to when.

Wind is like time,
Time is like wind,
A ride and a companion.

In the wind,
There is time, and in time,
The wind lives.

바람과 시간 (2)

바람은 시간처럼
어디선가 어디론지
불어와서 불려 가지

시간은 바람처럼
언제부터 언제까지
흘러오고 흘러가리

바람은 사간처럼
시간은 바람처럼
올라타고 사귀는 거야

바람 안에
시간이 있고 시간
안에 바람이 살리

Intuition

(1)

I can't see it, hear it, or even feel it,
But a feeling seeps in from
somewhere.
There must be a wireless connection,
We've been connected for a long
time,
But we just live on, not knowing it.

(2)

Where do I go after crossing the
bridge?
Since it's embedded in my body,
mind, and soul.
I cross it instinctively and reflexively,
Not even realizing where my feet are
going,
Living without even realizing
the bridge is there.

(3)

Whether it's superficial or
fundamental,
Urgent things are communicated
through intuition.
The direct wireless communication
line will be activated,
The sender will forward countless
messages,
The receiver will let them go or
ignore them.

육감

(1)

안 보여도 안 들려도 모르게
어디선가 스며드는 느낌이 있지
무선통신로가 분명히 있을 거리
오래전부터 연결되어 있는데
그저 그러려니 그걸 모르고 살리

(2)

다리를 건너 어디로 가지
몸과 마음과 혼에 배어
본능적으로 반사적으로
발 가는 줄도 모르며 건너리
다리가 있는 줄도 모르며 살리

(3)

피상적이든 근원적이든
긴급한 건 육감으로 소통하지
직통 무선통신로가 발동하리
발신자는 수없이 메시지를 보내리
수신자는 흘리거나 무시해버리리

Parallel Universe

The waves of April cover the world.
On land, water, and in the sky.
The flower waves rise from south to
north,
And the leaf waves spread from the
fields to the mountains.

Waves will give birth to waves and
raise them.
Everyone rushes on the waves.
The sun is busy riding the big wave,
And the earth seems to be struggling
with the small wave.

Do all waves sail without destination?
Do they reach somewhere and
achieve something?
Are the passing events the assigned
duties?
Are the passing paths
the workplace?

Innumerable waves draw parallel
curves,
Unveiling everything that was hidden,
Tearing down what was blocked,
Creating parallel universes
and circulating them.

평행우주

사월 물결이 세상을 덮는다
땅길에도 물길에도 하늘길에도
꽃물결이 남에서 북으로 오르니
잎 물결은 들에서 산으로 퍼지지

물결이 물결을 낳고 키워가리
모두가 물결을 타고 내닫는다
태양은 큰 물결 타느라 여념 없고
지구는 애 물결도 버거운 모양이다

모든 물결은 정처 없는 항해인지
어딘가에 닿아 무언 갈 이루는지
지나가는 일이 바로 받은 임무인지
스쳐 가는 길이 바로 일터가 되는지

무수한 물결이 평행곡선을 그리며
가렸던 것들을 말끔히 벗겨내 가며
막혔던 것들을 시원히 헐어내 가며
평행우주를 이루어 순환시켜 가리

Epilogue

Evening Glow

The burning evening glow is
A glimpse of the dazzling tomorrow
Its wondrous hues and forms
Will change in amazing ways

In the eyes of every beholder
A blossoming tomorrow will be found
Before we know it
A cherished hope will come true

Every spectacle that moves the heart
Is a fleeting revelation of eternity
All rush to the sea where the sun
sets
To see it up close and in detail

에필로그

저녁노을

불타는 저녁노을은
눈부실 내일의 예시
신묘한 빛깔과 모습이
시시각각 놀랍게 변하리

바라보는 눈마다 그 안에서
피어나는 내일을 만나게 되리
어느 사이 저도 모르게
간절한 소망이 이루어지리

가슴을 흔드는 모든 장관은
영원을 알리는 찰나의 계시이지
좀 더 가까이서 자세히 보려
모두 해지는 바다로 몰려들지

About the Author
Lee Won-Ro

Poet as well as medical doctor (cardiologist), professor, chancellor of hospitals and university president, Lee Won-Ro`s career has been prominent in his brilliant literary activities along with his extensive experiences and contributions in medical science and practice.

Lee Won-Ro is the author of fifty poetry books along with eleven anthologies. He also published extensively including ten books related to medicine both for professionals and general readership.

Lee Won-Ro`s poetic world pursues the fundamental themes with profound aesthetic enthusiasm. His work combines wisdom and knowledge derived from his scientific background with his artistic power stemming from creative imagination and astute intuition.

글 쓴이
이원로

시인이자 의사(심장전문의), 교수, 명예의료원장, 전 대학교총장인 이원로 시인은 월간문학으로 등단, "빛과 소리를 넘어서", "햇빛 유난한 날에", "청진기와 망원경", "팬터마임", "피아니시모", "모자이크", "순간의 창", "바람의 지도", "우주의 배꼽", "시집가는 날", "시냅스", "기적은 어디에나", "화이부동", "신호추적자", "시간의 주름", "울림", "반딧불", "피리 부는 사람", "꽃눈 나라", "별들의 노래", "멈출 수 없는 강물", "섬광", "마중물", "진주 잡이", "춤의 소용돌이", "우주유영", "어찌 등을 미시나요", "불사조 행렬", "마침 좋은 때에", "나팔소리", "전야제", "타임랩스 파노라마", "장도의 서막", "새벽", "초점", "소리 벽화" "물결", "감사와 공감", "합창", "코로나 공황", "대화", "빨간 열매", "꽃과 별", "바람 소리", "우리집", "오늘 안의 내일", "파도의 터널", "찻잔과 바다", "타임 캡슐", "약속", "소생", "밤하늘", "초대장", "박수갈채", "회복의 눈빛", "DNA 안 은하수" 등 50권의 시집과 11권의 시선집을 출간했다. 시집 외에도 그는 전공분야의 교과서와 의학정보를 일반인들에게 쉽게 전달하기 위한 실용서를 여러 권 집필했다.

Lee Won-Ro`s verse embroiders refined tints and serene tones on the fabric of embellished words.

Poet Lee Won-Ro explores the universe in conjunction with his expertise in intellectual, affective and spiritual domains as a specialist in medicine and science to create his unique artistic world.

This book along with "Milky Way In DNA", "Signs of Recovery", "Applause", "Invitation", "Night Sky", "Revival", "The Promise", "Time Capsule", "The Tea Cup and the Sea", "The Tunnel of Waves", "Tomorrow Within Today", "Our Home", "The Sound of the Wind", "Flowers and Stars", "Red Berries", "Dialogue", "Corona Panic", "Chorus", "Waves", "Thanks and Empathy", "A Mural of Sounds", "Focal Point","Day Break", "Prelud to a Pigrimage","Rehearsal","TimeLapse Panorama", "Eve Celebration", "A Trumpet Call", "Right on Cue", "Why Do You Push My Back", "Space Walk", "Phoenix Parade", "The Vortex of Dances", "Pearling", "Priming Water", "A Glint of Light", "The River Unstoppable", "Song of

이원로 시인의 시 세계에는 생명의 근원적 주제에 대한 탐색이 담겨져 있다. 그의 작품은 과학과 의학에서 유래된 지혜와 지식을 배경으로 기민한 통찰력과 상상력을 동원하여 진실하고 아름답고 영원한 우주를 추구하고 있다. 그의 시는 순화된 색조와 우아한 운율의 언어로 예술적 동경을 수놓아간다.

이원로 시인은 과학과 의학전문가로서의 지성적, 감성적, 영적 경험을 바탕으로 그의 독특한 예술 세계를 개척해가고 있다.

이 시집을 비롯하여 "DNA 안 은하수", "회복의 눈빛", "초대장', "밤하는", "소생", "약속", "타임캡슐", "찻잔과 바다","파도의 터널","오늘 안의 내일", "우리집", "바람 소리", "꽃과 별", "빨간 열매", "대화", "코로나 공황", "합창", "물결", "감사와 공감", "소리 벽화", "초점", "새벽", "장도의 서막", "타임랩스 파노라마", "전야제","나팔소리","마침 좋은 때에", "어찌 등을 미시나요", "우주유영", "불사조 행렬", "춤의 소용돌이", "진주잡이", "마중물", "섬광", "멈출 수 없는 강물", "별들의 노래", "꽃눈 나라", "피리 부는 사람", "반딧불", "울림", "시집가는 날", "시냅스", "기적은 어디에나","화이부동", "신호추적자", "시간의 주름" 등은 아래에서 구입할 수 있다.

Stars", "The Land of Floral Buds", "A Flute Player", "The Glow of a Firefly", "Resonance", "Wrinkles in Time", "Wedding Day","Synapse". "Miracles are Everywhere", "Unity in Variety" and "Signal Hunter" are available at Amazon.com/author/leewonro or kdp.amazon.com/book shelf(paperbacks and e-books).

Amazon.com/author/leewonro와
kdp.amazon.com/bookshelf(paperbacks
and e-books)

Made in the USA
Monee, IL
19 September 2023

43003022R00090